Love Is

Not

A Three-
Letter Word

MIKE G. WILLIAMS

Other Books By Mike G. Williams

Turkey Soup For The Sarcastic Soul Vol 1

Turkey Soup For The Sarcastic Soul Vol 2

Life Happens: Shut Up, Smile, and Carry a Plunger

An Amateurs Guide To Skunk Repair

*Men Moved To Mars When Women Started
Killing The Ones On Venus*

———————————

Love Is Not A Three Letter Word

also available in Latin Spanish
www.FocusOnTheBanquet.com
or www.BanquetMoney.com

Dedication

For the past ten years I have spent my spring and fall speaking around the country for some amazing warriors who are engaged in a great battle. This book is dedicated to the Pregnancy Resource Centers and Youth Training organizations across the country who make victory come from less than perfect situations. I salute you. This book is part of my effort to truthfully educate students and reduce the number of students these organizations need to counsel each year.

Contents

Chapter 1

Jack & Jill

*The story I remember was that Jack and Jill went up
the hill to fetch a pail of water. Then Jack fell down
and pretended to sprain his ankle so that Jill would
sit by his side and kiss him.*

MGW

Let's talk about a guy named Jack (we have changed his name from Adam to Jack to protect his anonymity). One day Jack wakes up from a nap and begins meandering about in a really cool garden. He swings from the vines and roars with the lions. He is a regular Tarzan type dude for sure. *Kind of like Justin Beeber with the addition of muscles and facial hair!* Unfortunately, Jack was lonely. He wanted to find some creature who he could truly adore, and play with, and take care of, and do that for the rest of his life. Then one day, while swinging from a coconut palm, out of the corner of his eye, he catches the glimpse of a strange creature in the garden. This creature is very similar to him, but very different. It is beautiful! He moves in closer. He waves. He uses the world's first pick up line as he grunts out, "Now that I met you, nothing else matters." There you have it...the struggle was on...the quest had begun. From that point until now both man and woman have been looking to find a soul mate, a true partner, a genuine lover.

I am having a dilemma right now. How do I have an intelligent conversation about this subject, in your student language, without totally freaking out your parents and grandparents? Give your parents a break for a minute. They gave birth to you…they raised you the best they could…they have high hopes for your success…and they want to think that somehow your world is more like the world of *Little House On The Prairie* than it is like the world of *Jersey Shore*. So, I have got to talk to you about this. There are many students getting hurt out there. It's time we sat down and had a conversation like mature individuals.

I grew up in a conservative religious family. My Dad gave me "The Talk" by saying, "Son, you know that men… and ah…women…are ah…different. You know that right? Good. Now let's go shoot some guns or something." When I tell people that they laugh. Nevertheless, it is true. My parents' generation refused to talk about anything closely related to human sexuality. My mother would even whisper the word "pregnant" as if saying it at full volume would cause somebody else in the room to become pregnant. As far as health information, I was raised to believe that *crabs* were something you caught at the beach, and the clap was something you did after someone sang a song. Again, they had good intentions and high hopes for me, but were a little shy. Thus ignorance led to some interesting mistakes. Ignorance always does. That is why I am writing this book.

I need to apologize to you for a minute. Many of my own generation did a disservice to you. In our desire to correct the missing information of our parents generation, we opened the floodgates of misguided information. We made sexual information and misinformation very open and easily available to anyone at any age. I am not talking about your Science teacher Mr. Zamzo teaching a health class on the human body. I am talking about our cable television and high speed internet teaching us through Jersey Shore, Desperate House Wives, and YouTube. We have allowed our celebrities to disciple us in sexual misinformation. Now certainly I think that you students (even at a middle school level) qualify to know this stuff. It was just a few hundred years ago that you would have been preparing for a wedding and full time job at your age. However, times were different then.

We didn't have things like…indoor plumbing and electricity. However, we certainly did have sex and you are fully aware of that.

Sometimes in schools I will say, "I am not against sex, for we are all here because somebody had it." That always brings "moans" from the crowd. Why? If sex is natural why would you be embarrassed by realizing that you came from it? Get over it. Seriously, if you want to be treated like adults, well you know...

I have heard it said by some students, "Our parents got to experiment with sex. Why shouldn't we?" Good point! Let's run with that. I know a kid who experimented with drinking battery acid to get a buzz—you gonna try that? Why not? I know a kid who after one of my school talks set his arm on fire trying to duplicate something I talked about. Are you going to try that? Why not? I know people who have jumped off bridges, smoked dog poop, huffed gasoline, and held up banks. Are you going to try all those? Why not? Because at some point an intelligent person realizes that they can learn from the mistakes of others. *Possibly some people can't, I don't posses an IQ tester at the moment to know for sure.* My good friend says, "This is why we have short busses and most likely always will." Unfortunately even education can't fix stupid. So if that is your category, simply read this book for the ten dollars your mom or grandmother promised you if you would read it, and get a few laughs at the rest of us.

As I progress in this paperback letter to you, I am going to get very-very real. This book is not for wimps. I will be brief for the sake of propriety, and so your parents will let you read this book. I realized I needed to write this book when my then six year old son came home from kindergarten asking sexual questions that I had to look up on the internet. I don't remember having that knowledge when I was in Kindergarten. *Maybe that is why my voice didn't change until I was fourteen.* Now he was just repeating something that he had heard, but it was a real wake up call for my wife and me. It was upon hearing this that I knew we had a situation to contend with.

This book is explains how to find genuine love. It is not primarily about whether it is right or wrong to have premarital sex. I believe sexual impulses are God given. I also believe that they have unfortunately been improperly supercharged. For example…God gave us potatoes…but did He intend for us to eat so many potato chips that we ended up looking like a potato, or becoming a couch potato? I want to focus our discussion to genuine love. However, I will include much about sex as a very related topic.

In this book I intend to prove that most students settle for sex when they are looking for genuine love. I am not blaming them. It is only natural that they do this because years of media has programmed them to believe that sex and love are virtually the same thing. A wise student will see past the deception and reach for that which is genuinely valuable. Sex in is not evil, it was created by God. However, sex at the wrong time can pollute our ability to achieve real love.

Chapter 2

Who's Afraid Of
The Big Bad Wolf?

You can't buy love, but you can pay heavily for it.
Henny Youngman

I don't think scare tactics work anymore. If scare tactics worked, none of us would have inhaled a cigarette, texted while driving, or watched Scream 4. We are students, we are immortal! None of us think that we would be the one to get any dreaded disease anyway. I know that I certainly would not! Diseases are for the loser, low life junkies, and people from the other side of town. *This disease stuff is for people who shop at Wal-mart after midnight and people who wear purple tube tops. You know the ones I'm referring too.*

If fear tactics worked nobody would put a crack pipe between their soon to be rotting teeth and nobody would put a needle in their arm for the first time. I don't think that fear tactics work in much of anything. Why? We, by nature love and admire risk takers! We love the Jackass videos. We applaud the guy who goes rock climbing by himself and ends up cutting his arm off. We cheer the athlete who risks life and limb to do what nobody else has done. If that athlete dies we say, "Well at least he died doing what he loved." We all feel that within us is the ability to have luck always on our side. We somehow have bought into the vagabond belief that *the odds will always be in our favor.* We believe that we could have won the Hunger Games.

When some abstinence speaker delivers a rapid run down the list of STD's, we are all amazed at the number of STD's there are. You've got Bacterial Vaginosis, Chlamydia, Gonorrhea, Viral Hepatitis, Genital Herpes, Human Papilloma Virus (HPV), Pelvic Inflammatory Disease (PID), Syphilis, Trichomoniasis, Chancroid, Lymphogranuloma Venereum (LGV), Pubic Lice (Crabs), Scabies, and a few more. *Some I cannot spell or pronounce like funkywumpus (okay I made that last one up).*

Of course we didn't even list HIV/AIDS, now did we? Who's afraid of HIV anymore? Magic Johnson has lived a long time with that. So why fear that? If you have millions of dollars for special treatment, you could live twenty or more years with that. At our age, that is a lifetime. Let me tell you, if you have ever had to sit in a room and help a mom tell her daughter that she was going to die from AIDS, you might see it a different way. But most likely you will never have to do that.

In the past fifty years we have gone from knowing of only four STD's, most of which were brought home from an unpopular war in Vietnam, to a current cornucopia of almost commonplace life threatening, itchy, scratchy, oozing, runny, deadly, painful, transmittable, life long illness. We have even changed the name of STD's (Sexually Transmitted Diseases) to STI's (Sexually Transmitted Infections) because infections seem much easier to treat. An STI is simply more palatable. Doesn't an infection simply require a few weeks of Penicillin? The word "disease" seems so permanent, but an infection is like a common cold. Big deal! *People die of disease, but people get to take Nyquil, eat chicken soup, and stay home from school if they have an infection.*

Seriously, how many people really get these STI's? Could it be about twenty-five percent? That means that seventy-five percent don't get anything! Excellent! What loser can't beat a twenty-five percent chance? Who wouldn't bet their life on that? Now of course that is based on one individual encounter. If you multiply the partners by four and do the math, you now have about a 91% chance of getting some type of STD, STI, or an STWhatever. *We can all hope it will be a small one that can just be treated with monthly ointment for the rest of your life. I'm sure the outbreaks are really over dramatized.*

According to the U.S. Government Center For Disease Control (CDC), the ages 14 to 24 represent 25% of all newly reported STI's. If you do the math on this group being less sexually active than some other demographics, the risk is very scary, though I am sure it is not for us! No way! We are invincible! We know that we aren't drug users or dirty white trash. We are clean, recently showered, middle class students who wear deodorant. We can afford protection. Maybe the school nurse provides them for us for free. Maybe we get them from Planned Parenthood. Maybe someone in our own family gives them to us. We are not afraid of the big bad wolf, at least not enough to cause us to change anything.

Now stop! This book is not about STD's or STI's or any other acrostic that can kill you. This book is about genuine love. Your grandmother might wonder why a student would risk their health these days. It is simple, because they are looking for real love. I want you to make decisions about your future based on truth and not on hormones and hunger. I want you to date and mate smart.

Chapter 3

So What Are You Really Worth?

I wanted to marry her from the first moment I saw the
moonlight shining on the barrel of her father's shotgun.

Rich Praytor

There has been much emphasis in past years about personal value and self-worth. Though you might look at your brother or sister and jest that they are worthless, we know that we all have a value. We are taught to value every person individually, especially if they were born within our U.S. held territories. We are also taught to value ourselves. Do you have a value? Do you think others could put a value on you? What in dollar amounts do you think you are worth? Give it a guess. If we are valued by the pound like meat, I may be worth more than most of you. *I'm just saying this is where we husky guys have a strategic weight advantage. Apart from your total value as a human, did you ever put a value on your varied individual parts? What is your right arm worth? Left leg? Pinky finger?*

Sometimes I get to speak to small classrooms filled with awesome students. I like to get them thinking. Although this book is not about the value of purity, I would like to chase a rapidly hopping illustration for three short paragraphs. I presented this interesting argument about premarital sex to a group of students one afternoon just for fun. I would love to know what you think about my premise.

It was only a few years ago when Americans watched in amazement as Natalie Dylan (a fictitious name) auctioned her own virginity online for a reported 3.7 million dollars. Following suite, thousands of miles away, Alina Percea (I'm sure also a fictitious name was used) who needed to pay for her computing degree who auctioned her virginity online to a 45 year old Italian man for just over thirteen-thousand dollars. Yes, these and many other girls have auctioned their virginity on the open market. *Yep, they just put it all out there on Ebay!* So if you were to put your own value (virginity alone) at midway between those two girls, your intimacy and one particular unexperienced body part is worth approximately two-million dollars. That is an awful lot of money. Think about it, you women are all millionaires. On a side note, for a world that says they value experience, they certainly don't pay the same for it. When experience (you know what I mean by that) is fifty bucks an hour and inexperience (virginity) is millions of dollars an hour, it does not make sense. By the way, guys' personal parts have not fetched a large price on any auction sites. Sorry guys.

It amazes me that the high school girl who would not trust a boyfriend enough to loan him twenty bucks would give that same boy a two million dollar item with no con- tract for repayment. Especially when it is the girl's only two million dollar part to give. I think any girl who has already given themselves away needs to send that person a bill. They should at least be on a small monthly payment plan. Maybe a dollar a day for the next two million days? I'm just thinking? Get a lawyer. Cash value is due you today.

My argument, which of course is ludicrous, was simply this; if you are going to offer up one of your most valuable assets, you might want to consider online auctions before donating it to some high school friend who will not remember your name in two years. Again, this book is not an argument for or against sex. It is about genuine love. So let's just move on to one final argument that I will [not] attempt to prove in this book.

Chapter 4

Missing Stick People Chart

I'm not good at math.
I can't even work a calculator well.

Paul Aldrich

Have you seen the sexual partner stick figure chart? Do you know the one I'm talking about? The stick figure chart that says if you have sex with this many people and they have had sex with this many people, then you have technically had sex with like a billion people. *Those charts make it seem like our private parts have served more people than a McDonald's!* One girl told me, "I don't like those charts. They make us feel like tramps." You are not tramps. You are simply trying to find love in a world that told you that sex is love. If you fell for that lie that sex is love, don't feel embarrassed. The media has been telling you that sex is love for many years. You (and I) have been technologically brainwashed. You (and I) are not alone. So has most of your family, friends, neighbors, police officers, rock stars, athletes, and even clergy. We are all victims of this seemingly planned misdirection of love.

When you have that crazy stick figure chart it makes intimacy just seem rather nasty. It reduces sex to something from a multi-level marketing business presentation. If I tell two people and they tell two people and they tell two people, before you know it the story will be around the world. Throw in a few shares on Facebook and a tweet or two, and you now have a reputation as big as Paris Hilton's social network. If a person was charging money for intimacy instead of just getting a free dinner, they might just be put in jail for this kind of enterprise. *I'm just saying.* Nevertheless, I don't need to dwell here on this chart, it is not our real topic, we need to talk about love. So let's get on with it!

Chapter 5

Not A Three Letter Word

What's love got to do with it?
What's love but a second hand emotion?
Tina Turner

In 1985, Tina Turner won a ton of music awards with the release of song entitled *What's Love Got To Do With It?* I remember that song well. The airwaves played the mess out of it. It still rings in my mind many years later. So when you think about it, the LOVE word has been tossed around for a long time now. Someone said that 99.9% of every song on iTunes is about finding love, finding what we hope to be love, or a love gone bad. Humankind is infatuated with love. Unfortunately most of humankind does not really have any idea what love is.

Insanity is often defined as doing the same thing over and over again and hoping to get different results. Do you think that statement is correct? It seems a bit crazy to me that for a people so hung up on finding a satisfying love, and so notably not finding love, they continue to seek love in the same way as before. These human lemmings (A lemming a small furry animal known for following its family in charges off the side of cliffs) allow the [love ignorant] to define love for them. These musical artists who cannot find love in their own lives have somehow through the miracle of rhythm and lyric become the teachers of love to the masses. Is it any wonder nobody can find love? Is it any wonder that students and parents continue to ask the same compelling question Tina Turner did? Really…what's love got to do with it?

Stop! I want to suggest to you that we are defining love the wrong way. Unfortunately in most songs the LOVE word is used as a replacement for the word SEX. Thus, by sheer repetition, sex has been the definition of what most people call love. The musicians would use the word sex, but it just doesn't rhyme well. What rhymes with sex? Hex, vex, Tex-Mex, or maybe T-Rex. All words that you wouldn't usually find in a song about two people searching for intimacy! You hear people refer to sex as "making love" when they are truly only having sex. Think about it. Most people think that sex is love and love is sex. Are you tracking with me? There is no way, with any integrity that you can say that dropping your tighty-whities in a stinky middle school janitorial closet is love. Don't try. It won't play.

Now I am not against sex in any way. I know that most of you will rather enjoy it if you wait for the right time. Millions of people already know that. Nevertheless, calling sex by another name does not make it something other than what sex really is. Just because I call a "dog" a "cat" does not make it a cat. However, if you call a "dog" a "Cat" for long enough you can change the definition for the next generation. That is where you, my student friends, have been ripped off. You should stand up and protest. You should occupy music row and demand that they return the truth that they have taken from you. You should picket and protest. You need to march on Hollywood and demand that they define their terms more properly. Yes, LOVE exists. Yes, SEX exists. And they both can be enjoyed or endured simultaneously, but they are not the same thing.

Someone said, "Who cares what is what and which is which and if love is sex or sex is love?" That would be a valid point if all we needed in life was sex, but it is not. We were created to give genuine love and be genuinely loved. Loved! Truly and genuinely loved. Genuine love brings long term happiness and joy to our life. It last more than a ninety-second smile. I intend to prove to you that this sex versus love question is the primary question any student or any person for that matter must ask before they can find really good sex or really genuine love. Again, this is coming from a guy who is not anti-sex at all. I am very pro-sex.

Stop. Let me give you my definition of both words.

Sex: The physical act between two people whereby two people engage in the connection of body parts until one or both finish the experience with a completely natural and amazing feeling of momentary euphoria. It can happen between two strangers or two friends. It does not require love or even mutual consent. It requires only momentary infatuation at best or narcissistic sexual desire at worst.

Love: A never ending bond between two individuals whereby each consider themselves an intimate part of the other whether they are or are not experiencing physical touch at the time. This bond is so strong that the two involved may genuinely feel it would be better to die at the same time, for separation would be a torture beyond what they could bare. Love adores the other, looks to please the other, honestly compliments the other, thinks the best of the other, keeps their bodies reserved for the other, keeps their promises to the other. Genuine lovers engage in sexual acts as a way to experience unified euphoria, and unhindered expression of total commitment. For the genuine lover, intercourse is virtually a holy experience smiled upon by a Holy God.

Now which of the above do you want? Do you want sex or love? Both have sex involved, right? Which one fulfills the persons desire and need to have committed life-long genuine love? Which fulfills our desire to have someone who will be our closest never leaving friend? Which gives us someone who will hold our hand when we don't have the strength to hold our head up? Which one stays with the other in tough times? Which one does not walk away from the children they made together? Hmmm? Good questions.

Some might say, "Can you really have genuine love?" Yes, you can have love! There I said it! It can be achieved. The mediocrity myth is over. The truth is out. The cover has been blown. The banner has been lifted. The rabbit is out of the hat. The white smoke has come from the papal chimney! *Okay that last one may not have made sense to you unless you watch the news, sorry!* Without a doubt we know that there are people...on this planet...many...who [are] experiencing great love. So it is doable. It is achievable. Would you like to have that kind of love?

Chapter 6

Do You Believe In Velcro?

Without NASA we never would have had Velcro.
I'm sure glad we went to the moon.

Gordon Douglas

So how do we achieve this real love? Do we have to go to
E-Harmony and register online? Good question. Because the
truth is that many people try to achieve real love, and don't
achieve it. So we have people with good intentions who fail!
Ouch! It sure would be fantastic if everyone who worked hard
for real love would get real love. Working hard for anything
is only good if we are working in the right direction. I can
have a desire to go to Alaska, but if I attempt to get there by
pogo stick, maybe I might not reach the moose infested state.
Do you have hopes for me to make it? Even if I did make it,
I might not be suitable for anything once I finally got there.
Do you comprehend this illustration? I think you are smart
enough to understand. So if you want to have genuine love,
you are going to have to go about achieving it the right way.

Before we discuss how to have genuine love, let's talk
about ways to connect simple household items. *Stay with me
momentarily, I promise this will lead somewhere good.* First on
our list we have Velcro. Do you like Velcro? I like to take a big

piece of it and just connect and rip, connect and rip, connect and rip. I could go on doing that all night. I am a man, it does not take much to totally mesmerize me. I'll watch NASCAR for hours. Velcro offers a convenient hook up, and lasts until a little pressure is put in the opposite direction. Velcro does not create a bond between two objects, only a very temporary connection. The side effect is unfortunately that after being connected and disconnected many times, the velcro itself looses its own ability to connect at all. That is sad. *Now you know the Velcro Fairy Tale. The End...*

Many people, if not most, settle for Velcro love. Unfortunately, after a few years of connecting and disconnecting to another person or many persons, the ability of the *Velcro* love to hold us securely to each other is rather weak. This unfortunately is the kind of relationship that modern society has been recommending. You have been taught their version of Velcro love since you were old enough to understand the birds and the bees. You saw it on television. You saw it in hook ups. You saw it in dating sites. You saw it in *Friends With Benefits*. But it has failed miserably and the bodies are strewn by the hi-way in the wake of this tragic imitation of real love. Many of you have had to deal with the pain of broken families, which is very often the painful consequence of Velcro love. Do you want to have genuine love, or velcro love? That was a silly question. We know the answer.

Let me recap what I have said up to this point, and let's see if you would agree with it.

1. Sex is pleasurable, but it is not genuine love.
2. Anyone can have sex, and do so without giving or receiving genuine love.
3. Genuine love will (at a point) include sex, but has so much more to offer.
4. Desiring genuine love does not mean that you do not desire sex.

5. Many students are trying to experience love through non-working methods.
6. Sex very often ruins a young person's ability to ever attain genuine love.
7. A pogo stick is a bad way to get to Alaska.

Great, real, genuine, amazing love comes from a great bond. Bond? Like superglue. A bond is like a weld. It is metal being heated together until the metals melt together and there is hardly a place where you can see where they separate. Getting back to our household items, I often explain that a great bond of genuine love is like an epoxy glue. *Epoxy* glue is different from the *Elmer's paste* we used to eat as a child in kindergarten, or the *Elmer's glue* stick that we were allowed to use after we got big enough to know better than to eat it. An *epoxy* is strengthened not by it's exposure to air, rather by the combining of multiple ingredients, from multiple tubes. After all the ingredients are mixed, it is applied to two items that have been cleaned thoroughly, there is usually a drying time, but then…KAZAM…the bond that is formed is solid as a rock. Maybe even more solid than a rock.

Like the *epoxy* glue, there are multiple ingredients that need to go into your genuine love bond. These four ingredients when combined in equal proportions will form a lifelong bonded love and become the basis for a very happy, lifelong partnership. If either party leaves any of these ingredients out of their foundation they are dooming their relationship to trouble. I will let you in on a little secret; the good news is, one of the ingredients will eventually include great sex.

If you want genuine love and not just sex you are going to have to work on bonding. You are going to have to prepare yourself to truly bond, and you are going to commit yourself to not settling for sex when a great love is achievable. I know you can do it.

Chapter 7

Got Glue?

There is no remedy for love but to love more.
Henry David Thoreau

When you read the instructions on the back of the multiple epoxy glue tubes you will find that step one is preparation of the two items to be joined. Sometimes that means cleaning the item very well and giving time for the item you washed to fully dry. Sometimes it requires multiple passes of harsh sand paper to prepare the item to be bonded. If you were making a list of things you think would prepare someone to be bonded to you, what would that list include? Let me get right to the point. Would your list of lover preparation include the following statements?

1. I want my genuine lover to have experienced lots of sexual situations with lots of partners and thus bring lots of possible health variables into our bond.
2. I want my genuine lover to have many other sexual experiences that I will have to live up to as we grow old together.
3. I want my genuine lover to have watched hours of sexually explicit material for me to have to live up to in

future years. Remember, memories don't age as we do. Memories stay in their original time zone.

4. I want my genuine lover to be compared to super porn models, silicone implants, photoshop, and former relationships.

Or would your list include the following statements?

1. I want my genuine lover to have saved themselves for a genuine love.
2. I want my genuine lover to love me without constant comparison to others.
3. I want my genuine lover to be free from distractions from me.
4. I want to be in a relationship with my genuine lover with nothing to loose, nothing to prove, and nothing to hide.

So if there are certain [shall we say] desirable traits that you would consider as good preparation for your genuine lover to bond with you, would you put those preparatory conditions on yourself? It is a legitimate question. You would do well to be honest enough with yourself to answer the question.

Many people look to find a genuine lover to bring wholeness to their life. That is a big problem. It is like someone who is in a wheelchair thinking that if they could find a lover who can walk, then they could somehow miraculously walk. How crazy is that? Hurting people do not become un-hurting by connecting to someone else who appears to be a little more mentally stable than they are. Broken people link to others and carry their broken life into the life of another. If both parties are broken, the effect is only exacerbated. Doubled! Even squared! So if you want a real love, bonded love, love like I described earlier in Chapter 5, you are going to have to prepare to be bonded. Your future love interest is going to have to invest in the time it takes to prepare themselves to be bonded also. You will only have a bond as good as both parties are prepared to bond. A concrete block makes a great surface to bond with, unless the substance you are trying to bond to it is Jello pudding. Now you have a problem. *That is a shame because I really like Jello pudding.*

What do you have to do to get ready to experience a good bond and thus a great love? How much time will you need to heal from past mistakes? How much preparation time? How much time do you and your genuine lover need to prepare yourself for a good bonding to take place? Will it be hours? Days? Weeks? Months? Years?

Some might not want to take the time it takes to have a great bond. That is a shame because everyone will spend their life either messing up in love, or enjoying love. We will all share the preparation time factor. Your choice is whether you want to spend the time victorious or miserable. The choice is up to you. I can't fix stupid. However, you can.

Chapter **8**

Secret Ingredients

Those who love deeply never grow old; they may die
of old age, but they die young.
A.W. Pinero

All four of these ingredients in this bonding cement of love are very similar. In fact, I am going to use the word LOVE as an acrostic to help you remember each ingredient in the bonding process. *There is nothing like a good acrostic to jog the memory.* We will delve into the Greek vernacular a bit to seem intelligent, but Greek words *(Eros, Philia, Storge, Agape)* are not the magic of the ingredients. We could say them in English, Spanish, French, German, Chinese, or Polish. Whatever the language, it all boils down to a few simple ingredients, applied to a well prepared surface, that creates a great love.

The more time two people spend developing each of these ingredients will directly effect the outcome of your bond. If you rush any of these ingredients, or try to rush through the preparation, you will most likely ruin the cake and have to start all over. You will need equal amounts of each ingredient, and it will take equal time to properly prepare each ingredient. Remember, when you do things right, time is on your side. When you do things wrong, time becomes you enemy. You will waste more time messing up on love than you will from getting it right. So do you want to spend your time winning or loosing? The choice is yours. This is one recipe where patience truly is a virtue.

> *On the first day of the new school year I was sitting at my desk minding my own business, when a girl named Cari walked into the class…Cari wasn't a new student, but something happened over the summer and I said to myself, "I gotta get me one of those."*
> Kyle Idleman, Not A Fan

L

Look At That!
Ingredient - EROS

Eros is a love ingredient that can best be described as adoration, or "WOW…look at that!" It is that quickening of the spirit, the pitter-patter of the heart, that uncontrollable infatuation that one has when they see that special someone. Usually nobody else sees that person the same way, or at least are not enamored in the same way long term. It happens in a moment and it is lived out in long term adoration. You can't keep your eyes off of them. Everything about them intrigues you. You are enamored. I would call it worship. I call it that because it is the same feeling we express as we sing songs of adoration to our God. And when you are in the throws of Eros you are blind to everything else. This is a must have ingredient in a great bond…and subsequent great marriage. For our discussion, *Eros* is summed up in the statement: *Look at that!* Have you ever experienced this?

Eros is an ingredient that allows you to look at your lover in three years, or thirty years and still be emotionally stirred by their presence. You may think this is silly at your age, but when you are old, you will want to look across the table at someone you adore rather than tolerate. *Eros* develops well alongside the next ingredient. Take time stirring them together as long as possible. Why? To see if the *Eros* goes away! If it goes away—you can't ever achieve genuine love. Don't get beyond these individual ingredients until you have thoroughly mixed (experienced) them well, and for a faithful amount of time.

0

Our Commonality
Ingredient - PHILIA

Philia is a love ingredient that is best described as commonality, fellowship, and shared interest. It is the commonality you find with another in things you like to do, hobbies, activities, dreams you share, and adventures you take together. It is friendship love. But don't let that scare you. If you are going to have a great marriage you are going to be great friends with your spouse. *Without this you are merely sleeping with the enemy.* This is where the basis for lifelong mutual interest will keep you united in your conversation for a lifetime. Without developing shared interest and conversation there will be little to talk about in future years other than which divorce attorney to use, and that is not enough to make a relationship great. Trust me on this one. For our discussion *Philia* will be summed up in what I call: *Our Commonality.* Do you have this in your current hook-up?

Philia is that love that makes two people want to be together everyday for eternity. It is that deep friendship that means you will share common interests in life and laughter. So mix *Eros* and *Philia* for a while. A good while. This is not the time to add sex into the mix. In fact, sex at this point will pollute your recipe. Sex will make you skip the next ingredient and rush into a half love. It will ultimately leave you on the side of the love road looking for a kitchen to try cooking again. Mix these two ingredients as long as you can.

I love it when I am at a wedding and I hear the couple say, "Today I marry my best friend." When I hear that, and when it is really true, I know this is a marriage that has a chance to last.

V

Vulnerably Safe
Ingredient - STORGE

Storge is a love ingredient best described as trust love. It is revealed as we reach the point in a relationship that we share the innermost desires and fears of our hearts. It develops as we allow ourselves to be vulnerable enough to reveal the flaws in our self without the fear of rejection. *Storge* doesn't come overnight. It can't be achieved until the first two love types are well developed. This is the most often overlooked type of love. But without it, your marriage is doomed to divorce as time plays its nasty tricks on our bodies and health. I often refer to this as the love type that allows a spouse to sit for hours holding the hand of their beloved in those occasionally tragic golden years of a relationship. This is the love that says without audible words, "Don't worry…you wont die alone. I'm here. I'm holding your hand." For our discussion we will simply consider *Storge* under the heading: *Vulnerably Safe*. Do you have this?

This love type comes naturally for females, but it takes time to develop in males. Unfortunately many males (and some females) never develop it. This is the person you want to stay away from. They will leave you when times get rough, when the children get bothersome, when the Doctor says you might not remain in the same condition you are today. You must stay long enough in the development of this ingredient to know if you both have it for each other. There is no quick test for this. There is no swab for the tongue, and no rubber glove test. You will see it in the way your lover comforts you after you have been together for a while. Sex will pervert this. Some people will fake *Storge* to keep sex. So if sex is not in play, it can't be a distraction to Storge.

This natural development of our genuine love is now naturally calling out for the development of *Storge*. The *adoration* and *common interest* (lived out in time spent together) will naturally put you and your potential great lover in an easy place to be vulnerably honest with each other. If this does not happen, wait until it happens naturally. If you mix the first two ingredients together, and wait a while, it will happen, if it is supposed to happen. You know—written in the stars!

I don't cry at weddings, I am a man. I did at this one, but only just a little. I heard the young bride say to her spouse, "I will go where you go, your family will be my family, and when you die, I will die too, and be buried there along side of you." Wow! Only *Storge* can live that out. If they have this ingredient, they will not only survive, they will thrive.

E

Everlasting Promise
Ingredient - AGAPE

Agape is a love ingredient that could be best described as an everlasting promise. Covenant love is how some describe it! I know that sounds so cold and unromantic. Look, not every ingredient is tasty until it is mixed with the others. *Have patience my aspiring love chef.* Now we live in an age where contracts are made to be broken, or at least that is what the attorneys would have us to believe. *Agape* love is a heart given promise to love until death do us part. It is a signed contract promising to our lover (legally called a spouse) that we will give ourselves exclusively unto them, mind, body, and emotions. *No debates! No questions! No future re-negotiations!* It is witnessed best in the marriage ceremony in front of people who will hold us accountable to it, and lived out in a lifelong commitment to each other. *Agape* is often referred to as the religious type love. It is a choosing to love eternally. For our discussion, our acrostic, and for our ability to remember it, we will call it: *Everlasting Promise.*

Agape is lived out in the legal ceremony that calls us back to remember the promises made in the earlier ingredients even when we are not in a good emotional condition to do so. *Agape* is designed to make us stop and think before we do something stupid that would hurt our true and genuine love. You see even genuine lovers make stupid mistakes at times, and need time to realize it. Our love contract will help us always remember the reality of our genuine love and pull us back into recommitting to cooking up more great meals in the future. My friend asked me to just blurt out a one word description of Agape. I said, "Marriage-Ceremony!" I know it was two words, but I did dash them together. *I'm rather inventive when I have to be.*

You have a quick question, right? "Yes, when do we get have sex?" Good question. The answer is whenever you want to as long as you are of legal age. That is your choice. It always has been. Nobody has ever not had sex because they were waiting on *my* permission. HOWEVER…I might suggest that having sex while either of the first three ingredients are being put together can mess up your opportunity to attain genuine love. What happens when you put a cake in the oven before you put the eggs in the batter? You ruin your own cake. I will give you a suggestion for the sex part in a few more minutes, I hope you can wait that long.

L.O.V.E.
L - Look At That!
O - Our Commonality
V - Vulnerably Safe
E - Everlasting Promise

4 Ingredients applied to well prepared surfaces =
GENUINE LOVE

Yes…all you need is *L, O, V, and E* to have a great love (and phenomenal marriage). However, many people enter into sexual relationships without having all the key ingredients of real love. They may have the *Look At That—Infatuation Factor* going on, but they tossed sex into the recipe before it was time. They may have even chosen to get legally married so they could have what they believed was religiously legal sex. However, without all four loves solidly in place, their bonding glue will never dry, and their love will struggle.

Some overtly spiritual people might say that all we need is Agape love. They say, "If it is good enough for God it should be all we need." *It only takes a few minutes of good searching the Bible and real life to find out that these people have been out in the sun to long and have never read the Song of Solomon.* You need all of these love types to secure lifelong happiness in marriage. All of these love types are designed to gel and harden into an awesome bond that is culminated in a great love, a great marriage, and a totally awesome sex life.

While I'm here I need to re-mention that sex alone, good sex, great sex, will not make up for any missing steps in your bonding experience. Understand that you can put all the gas you want into the car…but if the engine is not running right…it is not gonna' run! I mention this because *some* people might think *some* teachers like myself are anti-sex. No way. I remind you again that I am pro sex! I believe in it, love it, and enjoy it. I also know that sex is not love by any shape of the imagination, and love is really what you want.

The term [making love] has been totally perverted by the media. Sex is sex. I believe God designed it. He implemented it. He smiles upon it within a fully bonded relationship (all four ingredients). So don't hear [anti-sex] in any way. It is good. Participate as often as you can within the confines of a fully completed recipe. It is healthy for you. Not only will it allow you to burn off that extra helping of mashed potatoes you had for supper, but studies show that if done often enough will reduce mens' risk of certain types of cancer. Within marital confines—get busy. Look into the eyes of your spouse and share intimacy.

I sat yesterday afternoon in a very hot and deplorable prison in the Dominican Republic. I sat across from an English speaking prisoner. He is currently in his ninth year of incarceration for a crime that would have gotten him probation in the United States. He told me about the week of his arrest. His wife flew from England to see him in that prison cell one week after she had given birth to their youngest child. She was unaware of his criminal activity. It was truly his first crime, and he did it to get the family out of debt. He explained to her that he was expecting to receive a twenty year sentence. He told her that he desired her to be free to marry again and find someone to be a husband to her and a father for their six children. Her response moved him then, and moves me now. She said, "I took you for better or for worse. I will be waiting when you get out if that takes twenty years." Now nine years into this sentence they still talk every night on the phone across the ocean. They look forward to the day they will be reunited. Wow, now that is *Storge* in action, that is a genuine love. That is the kind of love we all want.

Chapter 9

Side Effects Of Soup

Side effects are Gods way of reminding us that we can only partially fix things.
T.J. Foltz

Now this teaching comes with an interesting and positive little catch. I would call them side effects. We are all familiar with those. Every one of these love types bring to a relationship a different quality with them. To miss any ingredient along the way is to miss the fullness of a great love and miss the awesomeness of a great bond. Hear these next sentences very well. The percentage of time one spends in each of these four ingredients of love will determine the percentage of time that will be spent enjoying that ingredient during marriage. Many people skip through the four ingredients so fast they do not allow any type of love to really take root in their relationship.

For instance those who rush through the *Philia* (commonality) portion of your relational development will find that they will be married, and bonded to a stranger. They may adore this person who is a social stranger to them. They will live separate lives only to join in the bedroom from time to time to live out that portion of their union.Unfortunately the greater part their life will be lived out married, but lonely.

Secular media has told us all we need to have is *Eros*…and get into bed…quickly. It messes up your recipe. Societal norms have encouraged us to *get intimate* with our friends. You students call it, "Friends With Benefits." This horribly consequential *FWB* teaches us to find someone we enjoy being around and share mutual sexual pleasures the way you would share a round of golf. It may seem really convenient, but it leads to a never-ending search for real love.

Nominated for a 2011 Teen Choice Award, the movie *Friends With Benefits* put Justin Timberlake and Mila Kunis in just such a situation. The story led you to believe that friends who share sexually will fall in love and have that connection needed to experience genuine love. Many things that work in the movies don't work in real life. Nevertheless, they packed some of our favorite stars onto the screen and tapped into our brain with emotion. Be careful what you allow the movies to teach you. This same year Teen Choice gave us *Easy A, Just Go With It,* and *No Strings Attached* as the nominees for the year. Do the titles alone tell us enough about the underlying message? I know that the pure "hipness" of these movies and the million dollar advertising budgets will far outshine my ability to present *genuine love* in a competitive light. I'm sorry about that. However, I think some of you are smart enough to see through the hype. Some of you have been the victims of Fathers or Mothers who brought into your home the Hollywood love definition and that has left you in a broken family, with broken dreams, with broken finances, and you will never forget that. Some of you will not be able to afford college because one of your parents believed these lies a generation ago. It is likely that they did not have someone speaking truth to them. If they could do it over they would. Please think and stay smart! I think the movie should have been called *Friends With Consequences.*

Storge love (long term trust) has been all but written off in our self-serving narcissistic world. Without this ingredient in your bond, when the hard times come, and they will, your lover will be gone to another easier relationship. There are going to be many lonely old people in your generation. This is the exact reason many of my generation are now single parents, and you are in a single parent home. My heart goes out to all those in this situation.

I sat in a counseling session as the two argued out their problems. The problems all started when the guy's health had turned bad and he had to have part of his foot amputated. I listened to the wife of ten years finally blurt out the truth, "I just don't want to be married to a man in a wheelchair!" When I heard that statement, I knew the marriage was over. This home had *Eros*, it had *Philia*, it even had *Agape* (they had been legally married for ten years), but she did not have *Storge*. So when times got tough, she walked out.

As far as lifelong Agape commitments go, culture has taught us all to keep our options open. *Who needs Agape? We change our minds more often than we change our underwear.* I think that last line would make a great bumper sticker! Nevertheless, without lifelong commitment you find yourself wondering daily if you really have genuine love. You will live in fear. A great teacher of love once said, "Perfect love casteth out fear."

This skipping of, and/or rapidly rushing through any of these steps impedes our ability to really love and be fully loved. Skip the adoration time and you will find yourself not even attracted to your spouse about the middle of your first marital year. You will question what you saw in them to begin with. *"Was I drunk? I don't even drink. I must have been slipped a drug or something."* You will start looking at other possible lovers. Skip the commonality portion and you will find that you have nothing in common, and thus have nothing to talk about. I would hate to spend the rest of my life with someone I had nothing to say to. *I don't even like to sit next to someone on a plane flight that I have nothing in common with. That is why I sleep on planes a lot.* If you skip the trust building vulnerability step, you will live in fear of getting old, getting ill, getting bald, getting fat, getting ugly, getting your toe removed, getting poor, getting in a car wreck, or even being honest and vulnerable with your spouse. We all need at least one person we can be totally vulnerable with, and that really needs to be the one who is always going to be there for us. If you skip the *Everlasting Promise* (marriage contract) and you have nothing to keep you in the same room, much less the same house when you are having a bad day. Troubled times come, genuine covenant keeps you working together for success instead of calling a moving van or having an affair.

Chapter 10

Timing Is Everything

My talking alarm clock asked me what time it was.
I need a new clock.

David Dean

Yesterday I was making ramen noodles. It was one of those deluxe ramen noodle kits with a plastic bowl and two separate additive pouches, so don't feel sorry for me. I made them as I looked out my window at the beautiful Caribbean Ocean. *If I stand just right I can look across apartment 1B's porch and I can see the ocean outside their porch.* Life is good. I was watching a whale in the distance and got distracted from my noodle making. Woops! I added the water, poured in the magic ramen powder, and forgot to put the packet of freeze dried vegetables in. The wrong order, vegetables go in first. The wrong timing, flavor packet gets added after cooking. Now I have the wrong taste…and some really dry vegetables. Should two people have sex during this time? What do you think? *Remember, sex is like the ocean view through apartment 1B's porch, it will distract you from the task at hand and you will wind up with a dried up bag of veggies. Sex can do two things… it can destroy non-fully bonded people…or it brings genuinely bonded people closer together. Until you are fully bonded (1, 2, 3, and 4) sex will tear up your relationship.*

Your genuine real love scenario can only be accomplished in time. There is no microwavable love potions. The understanding of time is different for everybody. My four year old thinks that waiting more than thirty-seconds for anything is way too long. My fifteen year old son believes that anything that takes over a minute is a task worthy of sainthood. The high speed internet is always too slow for him. So is it any wonder that your generation struggled with waiting for anything? For that I apologize. We set you up for hardship. We taught you that anything can be achieved faster if you just turn up the juice. That will not work for love. There is no way you can rush these ingredients. There is no micro- wave-love. *There is however love with garlic cheese crust available at Pizza Hut.*

Time could perhaps be listed as a secret ingredient we did not list, but it is implied. For in this love soup we are making, problems in relationships show up with time. It is the time factor that tells you six months into your relationship that this person you are attracted to is a total dipstick! It is the time factor that forces your possible mate to be themselves, for real, and without pretense. Sometimes when you see the real and genuine you are smart enough to realize that you don't want to be fully in love with that Dr. Jekyll and Mr. Hyde. Yes, time can be your best friend. I guarantee you that five years into a bad relationship, with a spouse that won't come home at night, or help take care of the kids, or pay the rent, or get a job, or put the game controller down, and you will wish you would have taken the time to figure this one out.

The older you get the lower your standards get. I used to be so picky. Oh, when I get married he's going to be tall, handsome, rich...and I'm down to: registered voter. I'd marry a midget just for the handicapped parking.

Kathleen Madigan

How long is enough time? Good question. Do the math. When do you want to get married? When will you have saved enough money to tie the knot? "Two-years from now," you say. *Since Agape is really lived out in the one hour ceremony before you go on your honeymoon in Cleveland, you can simply divide the first three ingredients into twenty-four months. Let's see, twenty-four divided by three, carry the twelve, carry the common denominator, and I think you have eight or sixteen or 3a(24xy) in algebraic equation.* The answer is to spend the first twenty-four months on *Eros* and *Philia,* and *Storge* will naturally develop simultaneously in the later months. If you work on the first two, the second two will take care of themselves. Remember, the minute you bring sex into it, everything changes. When this happens your body will bypass reason and go straight for self-medication. This is where you will move from bonding to being simply each others pharmacist. You will play the bonding game, but your mind will play tricks on you. I understand how sex will control a male mind and lead that mind into manipulation. *A junkie will say anything, do anything, become anybody to get his or her fix.* I also know that sex will trick a female into thinking she is in genuine love, when there is really little more than a dash of *Eros* and little more. Time will become like a great wake up call. Unfortunately it is most often too late to keep a couple from becoming angry and bitter and divorced. Don't settle for less than the best. This bonding time is like a test drive for real life in thirty years.

Chapter 11

Back When Premarital Sex Was Allowed

I can't believe I just said that...You've got to be kidding!

When you get ready to go to the courthouse for that license, you might have to take a blood test. I have no idea why. But my wife and I did. Privacy Acts prevent them from telling any personal info about you, even to a future spouse. I think they just do it to scare people. A friend told me it used to be to keep people from marrying a close relative, sister, or cousin. How far back in the woods do some people live?

Here's a little trivia for you. Did you know that many cultures, including some ancient biblical cultures, required the couple to have sex before they were legally married? What? Really? They did. I'll bet they never told you that in Sunday School! Before you call your Pastor or Priest about this let me give you the whole dope on it. There was a big reason for it. The night before the actual ceremony the couple had to go and have intercourse on a clean sheet (sorry if this is grossing you out but you want to be treated like adults so deal with it). They had to bring the sheet to the priest to prove that in the act of the intercourse that the woman's hymen was broken, thus giving testimony that she had not been promiscuous before the marriage.

It was believed in those days, that if someone had given themselves sexually to another, they could never fully genuinely bond with someone else. For sex would have created a false bond between them and another. So, they had to prove to each other and the Priest that would perform the ceremony that they were wholly bondable. *Scary!* The leaders so wanted people to have a genuine love relationship, and they knew that previous sexual escapades could ruin those possibilities. So they required proof. This is gross. This is obscene. However, it was for the protection of the marriage.

Sex is an Oscar winning liar. It bonds you to people you do not even want to be bonded with. Sex has bonded the raped with the rapist, and the abused with the abuser. It is a strong bond—not a love bond—but a strong bond nonetheless. I'm not saying that this false bond cannot be broken. I feel like at this point I have to stop and say that if you have been a victim of sexual abuse, that there is healing for you. In God there is restoration. In the final chapter of this book we will address that healing and restoration. If this applies to you, please hold on.

We fear sexual activities because these activities will cover up character flaws that would cause you to reject a possible love mate under normal [sane] circumstances. It is kind of like beer. Get a little beer in you and you wake up married in Vegas. *Add sex to your dating—courtship—love recipe and you might just marry your cousin. Sex will make you wake up one morning married, wondering what in the world you have done, and saying, "So when did you get contact lenses? Wow, I didn't remember you having a uni-brow."* So to sum it up, sex can be a relationship killer. It most certainly will make you settle for less than the best person for you.

I want to add a very important note here. Some people believe they are saving themselves for [genuine] love by not having [real] sex. They believe they are somehow protecting themselves from having [real] sex by engaging in only limited [semi] sexual activity. That is the biggest joke I have heard since President Bill Clinton was supposedly 'not' having [real] sex with Monica Lewinski in the Oval office. Do you understand what I am talking about? Sexual activity carries with it much of the same baggage as [real] sex. Don't buy this bogus replacement theory, not that any wise student would.

Chapter 12

Let's All Purchase Protection

> *Think about this. Most condoms are made in China. China is the most overpopulated country in the world. Can we trust their quality control?*
> Jay Leno

Now when I say protection I am not talking about condoms. Let me give you an illustration of what I am talking about. Let's say that you just bought your dream car. What is it? You know what it is. Say it out loud. "My dream car is a _____ ." You bring it home from the car dealership, it is gorgeous. You park it out at the street and go to bed right? Right? I'll bet if I bought my brand new alpine white Mercedes convertible for two-hundred thousand dollars, I might spend another twenty- thousand and build a garage to keep it in. The garage is the protection on my investment.

Love has a garage. It is called a marriage certificate. It is *Agape*. It is long term commitment. It is a legal contract that declares if I am going to give you all of me, you and I must both promise to not walk away from the gift. If I am going to share with you my two-million dollar body part value, I want to know you are going to be there long term to appreciate it.

Marriage—*Agape*—Ceremony becomes the protection of your bond and genuine love. You don't have genuine love until you have un-coerced (You didn't have to force the other partner into it) legal paperwork. If your love interest is not willing to add the *Agape* certificate, they are unsure they are genuinely in love. RUN! RUN! RUN! This is your cue to scram. This is your writing in the sky from God to get out.

Let me give you an illustration of what *ceremony*, and thus *Agape*, brings to the genuine love table. You have heard of the Vikings, right? I am told that when they would land on the shoreline of any country they wanted to conquer, the first thing they would do is burn their own boats. They did not charge the enemy, they did not shoot their weapons, they burned their boats. Why? This was a demonstration to their enemy that they came to win or die, for they had no way to retreat even if they wanted to. The Viking warriors knew they had no option but to be victorious. A wedding ceremony is supposed to bring this kind of allegiance to a genuine love. It is a demonstration to everyone at the ceremony that you have eliminated your options to turn back. You are in this love to win or die.

Chapter 13

Do You Currently Have a MTD?

What you feed grows, what you starve dies. You never satisfy anything by feeding it, you only increase its appetite.
Dr. Crandall Miller

MTD's are tough to cure. Hear me out for a minute. Time will prove to you that sexually explicit material can be a real genuine love killer. Am I taking this overboard? I don't think so. Look, we all have questions about what the other sex really looks like. That is rather natural. I think National Geographic Television has answered much of that for us. If not, the Victoria Secret commercial just did. However, the constant feeding of yourself with sexually explicit material, is like snacking before a great big meal. Who wants to fill up on the dinner you cooked when you have been snacking all day on pizza? Real love waits for dinner! I call pornography a MTD (Mentally Transmitted Disease) and it is a real detriment to experiencing great love.

If you really want to have a great sex life within a great marriage you need to eliminate all pornography from your line of sight. No person can live up to what twelve script writers, five wide angle camera lenses, a *body* double, and what thousands of dollars of silicone can produce. Now when I say pornography I am not limiting that to internet nudity. The daytime soaps, the chick flicks, and the romance novels can be as detrimental to a female's sexual health as the magazines and internet are to a male. Anything that will make your sex life a *comparative act* is going to cost you more than you want to pay. Window shopping leads to disappointment.

If sex is not part of genuine love, why are we talking about something that hurts our sex life? Good question. I applaud those of you who were following closely enough to spot that. Good call. Well, here is my answer. Even though sex is not needed to create a great genuine love, it is a real party favorite after! So the protection of this area of your life is rather important. This is something you will want to share with your future spouse, let's not mess it up now. *When you are making one recipe it is dangerous to go looking through other Cook Books at other recipes!*

I can tell you about the couples I have counseled who have so filled their mind with pornography, that they were unable to complete sex with their lover. How insulting is that? "Sorry honey, you don't excite me enough to have complete sex with you. I will be looking thinking about others while I am with you." I certainly would not call that the words of a genuine lover. A true lover protects his/her mind for their spouse. There is no condom for the mind, and great sex begins with exclusivity of the mind. Your future sex life may hinge on what your eyes see today. Enough said.

Chapter 14

Can We Finish This Book And Collect Our Money?

Don't sacrifice the permanent on the altar of the temporary.

If you have found a way to stay clear of the influences of the media thus far I applaud you! Hip-hip hooray! Keep up the good work. Don't get lazy. Don't settle for less than what you can have, and that is a great love.

Remember, the media's influence is still inside you even if you have not acted on it. You have still been altered by it. It is a possible threat to you, like a Trojan horse virus. You must continue to fight it. Make yourself a promise to fight for genuine love. Write it on your wall. Buy a frame and put it on your desk. Promise yourself not to risk real love on the alter of lust or infatuation. Promise yourself that you will never do anything in a dating relationship that you would not want to tell your kids about in fifteen years, or your grandmother about on the phone as you are doing them.

Memorize the ingredients of genuine love and settle for no substitutes. You do not have to deny that sex is good, but you must learn to hold that precious gift for the person you are going to love forever. The greatest gift you could ever give your future spouse is the gift of saying, "I have saved my most intimate parts for you alone. I have not given away the great treasure to a BFF for a FWB hook up."

I know that right now your world is proclaiming sex, any way, any how. Then occasionally you hear some [out of touch] teacher type tell you that sex is evil, or bad. Others teach that sex is good as long as you are in love. Some teach abstinence. Some teach protection. I here I am trying to share a little long term truth. Believe me, one day you will thank me for the truth about genuine love. Truth has a way of proving itself.

Let's recap. Unwise students settle for sex when they are looking for genuine love. It is only natural that they do this because the media has programmed them to believe that sex and love are virtually the same thing. A wise student will see past the lie and reach for that which is genuinely valuable. Sex in itself is not evil, it was created by God. However, sex can pollute our ability to achieve real love.

The wise student will do whatever it takes to achieve genuine love and thus experience truly extraordinary sexual pleasures with the spouse of their dreams. I want you to make decisions about your future based on truth and not on hormones and hunger. I want you to date and mate smart. I want you to search until you find a genuine love, a love that will last. Don't settle for anything less!

I believe in you. You can make it. If you have found yourself to have gone too far already, please read the extra bonus chapter. I have asked the people who gave this book to you to prepare to run with the discussion from here. Be easy on them. They sometimes have a hard time talking about these subjects. Be nice. Help them through it.

Make love now and the good stuff will follow,

Mike G. Williams

When The Past Needs Fixing

Two different groups of students are addressed in this chapter. The first paragraph is for those who have been abused. The continuation of the chapter is for those who realize they have gone to far in relationships, and that of their own choosing. Many of you will find yourself in both categories.

I want to say this first and foremost...drum roll please... YOU CAN BE RESTORED TO NEW AGAIN. Some of you have been tragically hurt by people who should have protected you. My heart goes out for you. Don't let your past determine your future. I believe that in God there is restoration. Restoration is like a giant RESET button that returns us to normal. Nevertheless, that button sometimes takes months to find. But, if you are willing to be restored, I know that the Creator of all the universe is willing to restore you and give you a brand new start. Let me write sensitively here. For those of you who have been broken by someone that you should have been able to trust, please talk to a professional counselor today. Find a good Christian counselor and get well, and healed, and restored, and get reset.

Second group...drum roll again please...PAST MISTAKES DO NOT HAVE TO BE REPEATED! There I said it. Do you understand what I mean? Have you seen a U-turn sign? I saw a bumper sticker that read *God Allows U-Turns*. If He allows them, so can you. Don't let your past dictate your future. We have all had a past, but the future can be different if we want it badly enough.

Some of you may have been momentarily awakened by this book. For just a moment you came to your God-given senses and saw things outside of the blindfold. You are saying, "I've got a problem. I want genuine love, but there is a great amount of false bonding activity in my history and I don't know what to do about it." My heart breaks for you. The same way I hurt for the crack addict that wants to be free from the drug, but his mind tells him he needs more of the drug so very badly. Sex is a drug.

Honestly, sometimes I start out making chili, and I accidentally add the wrong ingredient, and then I add something to try and fix that, then I add something else to fix that added ingredient. Before it is over I end up making soup with spaghetti noodles poured over chicken fried rice. *Not what I had planned.* The problem for some of you in a relationship is that you may have [so] messed up your current attempt at love that you would be best to dump the dish into the trash and go get some new ingredients, and a new pan to cook it with. Salvaging a bad recipe rarely reaches full potential, and then you have to live with the sad soup, sometimes for the rest of your life. However, starting completely fresh is not always within our ability to do, and you know it. So let's examine a few love principles.

Are you currently in a trial love relationship? *Please know that they are all trial-relationships until you get the notary stamp on the marriage license!* Does your relationship have the first three ingredients of love fully in place and working well? Be honest! If not, you need to start the restoration process today. Only put off for tomorrow the things that don't matter. This is the most important thing on your horizon right now. Fix it. Fix it now. How do we do that?

She explained that her boyfriend is lazy, drinks too much, has a rap sheet longer than his arm, has no steady job, and he still lives with his mother! Now even with this list the girl says to me, "I know that my love can change him." Yes, the same love which has not accomplished any more transformation in the past six months other than to get him to switch from Budweiser to Bud Light. Sure you're going to change him! I wish there was a lottery ticket I could buy on the outcome of this one. I would be a millionaire next month.

MGW, from Men Moved To Mars

Here is the deal. If you are going to attempt to save a recipe that you have already messed up, you are not going to do that by continuing to put the wrong ingredients into it. If peppers are killing your soup, more peppers will not make it suddenly palatable. Let's be honest, sex (including semi-sexual activity) will falsify a bond. You see, sex does have some very strong emotionally bonding properties. Sex is a strong connector, but it is not a genuine love bond. You can bond to someone with nothing but sex, but in the end, all you have is sex and not genuine love!

Restoration comes first with a deep and honest desire to *really* fix it. Sometimes the cost of the repair is quite high. But then again, the cost of leaving things the way they are is higher. The cost to children who will be inevitably involved in the future breakup makes it unfathomable. *Well at least I would hope you find it unfathomable.* Certainly it is easier to cut our losses and start again. As creatures of habit, you will have the propensity to make the same mistakes again. So why not fix it now instead of waiting to fix it in the midst of your next failed attempt? You only have so many years. Why waste them in repeated misery?

We are *all* broken beings. Until we realize that we've got some problems of our own we will never be able to have a great marriage. If you are waiting on your lover to change and make you happy—get ready for some major lifelong disappointment. The key to having a great lover starts with being a great lover. You may think you are. Excellent! Get over it! We have all got some issues. Before you can help get the cataract out of your lovers eye, you need to get a some new glasses yourself. Remember that you need to be a whole person or you will kill your spouse trying to make them bring peace and happiness to your own life. It is time that you took responsibility for your own world. Can you admit that you have a few problems? If you said yes, read on. *If not, flush the toilet on this book and get a good Divorce Attorney on your speed dial.*

Let me make this a list. The fixing process begins as:

1. We realize that we have personally made mistakes and are truly sorry for them.
2. We commit to our own success in genuine love and the future of our family by making the hard choices now.
3. If your trial love interest will not commit to working on genuine love, we drop them like a hot potato. No deals, and no promises. Just a goodbye, and a wave as your car is accelerating in the other direction.
4. Stop having sexual intercourse, or sharing any other kind of sexual stimuli. Stop touching and start talking.
5. Build trust by the observation of how you control yourself. If you can't control your urges with each other, you most likely won't be able to control them when you're away at college either.
6. Make a time line. If this person is a possible genuine love, you can set a possible marriage date. Now you know how much time you have to work on the first two ingredients.

7. Commit to protecting the bond with legal paperwork before you risk the introduction of intercourse.
8. Commit yourself to prayer and the restorative power of God's Spirit. Read the Word of God and find encouragement to stand for truth when others around you are buying the lies.
9. Find a [sexually well] adult who will help you process this desire to be restored and reset.
10. Read this book over a few times to lock in the truth. Teach it to your friends. Only by teaching material do we come to fully master that material. *Become the Yoda of genuine love.*

Do or do not…there is no try.

Yoda

I believe in you. Others have made it. Others have won at this recipe for real genuine love. Don't settle for less than the real deal. Don't be the destroyer of your own possibilities. You can have a great lover, and a genuinely great love.

Open Letter For Parents & Grandparents

Dear Parents and Grandparents,

Let me be real honest with you. This book is designed to help you say what you may be having trouble saying about genuine love and human sexuality. However it is not my job to fix the entire problem. This book is a great starter. After your student reads it, the baton has been passed to you. Run baby, run with it!

You may have the tendency to think the information here is way too intimate for little Suzy or little Jimmy. If you do, I simply ask you to look at what is being posted on their Facebook, and what they receive in tweets. Then check out last year's Teen Choice Awards and Google the plot of the hit "TEEN" movies entitled *Friends With Benefits, Easy A, Just Go With It,* and *No Strings Attached.* They were all the top picks for teens, by teens. You might be greatly surprised at what their world knows and misunderstands about love and sex.

Last night, in preparation for this book I interviewed a student from small town America, who told me that when her mother had "The Talk" with her, she gave her mother some information that she did not know about modern intimacy. Times have changed. This book started for me when my Kindergarten age son came home with questions about what he heard the other kids talking about. I knew the world had changed and I needed to become pro-active about it.

We've allowed the world to hijack the beautiful and God-given and turn it into something tawdry. In our

*reaction to what the world has done with sex and love,
we have forgotten a biblical truth: Sex and passionate,
romantic love are God's ideas!...Why should we blush
over this subject? God devoted a whole book of the
Bible to present the context in which sexual love and
romance find their fullest expression.*

David Jeremiah

If parents and grandparents are afraid to approach these issues, there are rows of secular humanists who are ready to take your place. You need to be big enough to get over your own embarrassment and talk about these issues. Remember who brought the television home. This whole sexual revolution went south on our watch. We have responsibilities. We must deal with it!

*We survey people about their private sex lives, and
write manuals based on data gained by watching
people perform sex in a laboratory setting. To junior
high students we teach details of sexuality forbidden to
previous generations. At the same time, I know of no
greater failure among Christians than in presenting a
persuasive approach to sexuality. Outside the church,
people think of God as the great spoilsport of human
sexuality, not its inventor.*

Phillip Yancey

I am fifty years old. My generation didn't even talk about these subjects. I was somehow raised to believe that although God may have created sex, it was merely for procreation purposes and never meant to be celebrated, or enjoyed to any great degree. And...any truly morally proper or Christian person certainly never talked about it openly! How about you?

God designed us emotionally so that sex outside of marriage is not nearly as fulfilling or enjoyable as within a secure bond. Tragic damages occur when God's standard is violated.

Charles R. Swindoll

Sometimes our failure to give good clear information is similar to allowing our students to play on the railroad tracks with a train coming. It may be uncomfortable to talk about the big engine coming down the track, but somebody better do it. This generation needs to hear that the big engine is not bad, only dangerous if you get in front of it. Trains are good. Engines are good. Playing on the tracks is not safe. I know you are smart enough to see the comparison.

The Song Of Solomon is a convincing witness that men and women were created physically, emotionally, and spiritually to live in love.

Eugene Peterson

We sit with the kids and view relatively explicit stuff on television and we never talk about it. Forgive us, Lord, for letting the underwear commercials teach our children more about human sexuality than the church. My church taught me that the Song Of Solomon was a simply metaphor of God's love for the church. I read it myself...and there are naked people in there...and they are rather amorous. I don't think this book was about what my church originally told me it was about.

Sexual promiscuity has never been the established custom of any human society. Sex, sex, sex. Our culture is near the point of total saturation. The cesspool is running over.

J. Allan Peterson*

In our conservative shyness in talking candidly about sex, we inadvertently left the discussion in the hands of media moguls who hold neither our values, nor take responsibility for future generations. Let's take it back. Let's charge the gates of Hollywood with truth and propriety. Let's take back what belongs to the Creator and teach our children what was intended for them from the beginning.

I hope this book will become a great assistant for you. Pay your students ten dollars or fifty dollars to read it if you have to. It will be worth it. I have specifically limited religious language in this book, although these principles are definitely founded in Biblical truth and I will say that. I have written from this perspective because I do not want your students to feel this is overtly religious information which is limited to the overtly religious person. My goal is to relate to students on every level and save some lives and maybe even some futures.

For the next generation,

Mike G. Williams